Meg and Greg

A Duck in a Sock

Written by
Elspeth Rae and Rowena Rae

Illustrated by
Elisa Gutiérrez

ORCA BOOK PUBLISHERS

Published in Canada and the United States in 2020 by Orca Book Publishers.
orcabook.com

Library and Archives Canada Cataloguing in Publication
Title: A duck in a sock : with four phonics stories /
written by Elspeth Rae and Rowena Rae ; illustrated by Elisa Gutiérrez.
Names: Rae, Elspeth, 1973– author. | Rae, Rowena, author. | Gutiérrez, Elisa, 1972– illustrator.
Series: Rae, Elspeth, 1973– Meg and Greg ; bk. 1.
Description: Series statement: Meg and Greg ; book 1
Identifiers: Canadiana (print) 20190177195 | Canadiana (ebook) 20190177209 |
ISBN 9781459824904 (softcover) | ISBN 9781459824911 (PDF) | ISBN 9781459824928 (EPUB)
Subjects: LCSH: Reading—Phonetic method—Problems, exercises, etc. |
LCSH: Reading—Phonetic method—Study and teaching (Elementary) |
LCGFT: Instructional and educational works.
Classification: LCC PS8635.A39 D83 2020 | DDC jC813/.6—dc23

Library of Congress Control Number: 2019947371

Summary: This partially illustrated workbook, meant to be read by an advanced reader with a beginner reader or struggling reader, combines stories and exercises that focus on phonics and fostering literacy.

Orca Book Publishers is committed to reducing the consumption of nonrenewable resources in the production of our books. We make every effort to use materials that support a sustainable future.

Orca Book Publishers gratefully acknowledges the support for its publishing programs provided by the following agencies: the Government of Canada, the Canada Council for the Arts and the Province of British Columbia through the BC Arts Council and the Book Publishing Tax Credit.

Design and illustration by Elisa Gutiérrez

Printed and bound in Canada.

26 25 24 23 • 3 4 5 6

For our parents, Ann and Angus.
—E.R. and R.R.

For Mami y Papi, who nourished my love of reading and language.
—E.G.

In this book:

ck

sh

ch

th

Contents

How to read the stories in this book

Meg and Greg is a series of decodable phonics storybooks for children ages 6 to 9 who are struggling to learn how to read because of **dyslexia** or another language-based learning difficulty. The stories are designed for a child and an experienced reader to share the reading, as shown in the diagram above. A child feeling overwhelmed at reading sentences could start by reading only the illustration labels. More about this approach is on page 162.

What is included in these stories

The stories in this book are for a child who is familiar with all the **basic consonant sounds** (including **consonant blends**) and **short vowel sounds** and is ready for stories using words with the following letter combinations (**phonograms**): ***ck***, ***sh***, ***ch*** and ***th***. Each story in this book introduces one of these phonograms. The next story builds on the last one, so by the final story, a child is practicing all four phonograms.

The stories also use a few common words that can be tricky to sound out. These words are in the list to the right. The child you're reading with may need help with them. We recommend writing the words on a card that can double as a bookmark. If you're curious about why these common words can sometimes be tricky to read, flip to page 165.

Warning!

These words look little, but sometimes they can be tricky to read.

a
as, has
is, his
of
the
do, to
I
be, he, me, she, we
OK

This story introduces ***ck*** as in *dock* and *flick*. The letter combination (**phonogram**) ***ck*** is one way in English to spell the sound /k/. Other ways are ***c*** (*cat*), ***k*** (*kite*), ***ch*** (*echo*) and ***que*** (*antique*). Since the first two are **basic consonants**, they appear in this story. The second two are not included in the kid's text in this story.

The main thing to know about ***ck*** is that it only ever comes immediately after a **short vowel**, as in the words *blăck, pĕck, lĭck, rŏck and trŭck*. There are a few exceptions where /k/ is not spelled ***ck*** even after a short vowel, like *panic* and *trek*. We are careful not to use exceptions.

This story focuses on words with the sound /k/ spelled with ***ck***.

For a list of ***ck*** words, including all the ones used in this story, go to megandgregbooks.com.

A Duck in a Sock

A story featuring

Chapter 1

The **Duck** Pond

Meg and her best friend, Greg, loved going to their local park. Meg always brought birdseed as **snacks** to feed the **ducks** at the pond. Greg always brought his dog, **Rocket**, and threw **sticks** for him to fetch.

Meg fed **snacks** to the **ducks**.
Greg held a big **stick**.
stick
Rocket
peck
peck
ducks

OK, **Rocket**. **Pick** it up and run **back** to me!

Rocket was good at chasing **sticks**, but he was not so good at bringing them **back**. **Rocket** ran after Greg's **stick**. A minute later he ran **back** without the **stick**. He was dragging something else.

"What did **Rocket** find?" Meg asked.

"Looks like an old **jacket**," Greg said. "**Rocket**, I wish you would just bring **back** the **sticks**."

Greg saw another good **stick** under a **rock**. He bent down to get it and noticed a bag **stuck** under the **stick**.

Greg tried to lift the **rock** to get them both out.

backpack
ducks
Meg . . .
help me lift
the **rock**.
bucket
rock
stick

It's a
zip-**lock** bag!
zip-lock
bag

It has
nickels
in it.

Meg jingled the coins in the zip-**lock** bag. "**Lucky** you!" she said. "Looks like *lots* of **nickels**!"

Greg dumped out the **nickels** and started counting. Meg turned **back** to the **flock** of **ducks** and threw them more **snacks**.

"Woof! Woof!"

Meg looked up to see why **Rocket** was barking, but it wasn't **Rocket**. A big **black**-spotted dog was chasing **ducks** near a **dock** on the other side of the pond. As Meg watched, the dog grabbed a **duck** in his mouth.

dock

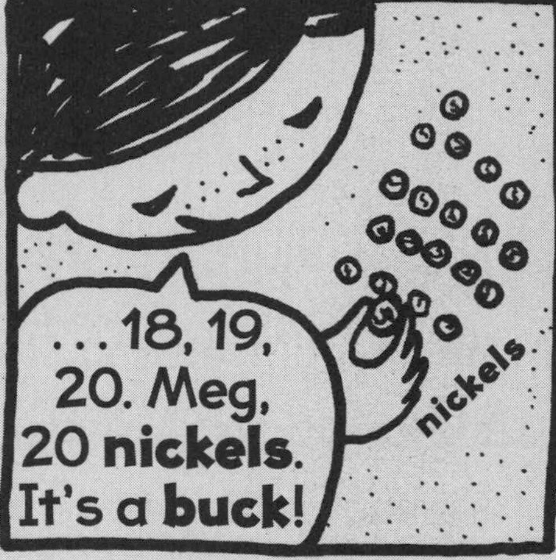

Meg and **Rocket** ran to the **dock**.

Chapter 2

On the **Dock**

Rocket barked and ran ahead of Meg. The **black**-spotted dog stood next to the pond. He held a small **duck** in his mouth! The **duckling** flapped its wings, but the dog held it firmly.

Meg got closer. "Stop that! Let the **duck** go!" she shouted. The dog growled and **backed** away from her. He stepped onto the **dock**.

Greg ran to the **dock** to help Meg.
Bad dog! Drop the **duck**!
Rocket
duck
dock

The wooden **dock** was old. It had long **cracks**, and parts of it dipped under the water.

Meg didn't care. She stepped onto the **dock** and walked toward the **black**-spotted dog. The dog growled again and **backed** away from Meg.

The big dog went **back** . . . and **back** . . .
and *plop*! He fell off the **dock**.
Just as he fell, he let the **duck** drop.

Meg ran to the **duck**.

"Poor little **duck**!" Meg said. "Greg, come and see."

"Uh, Meg," Greg said. "The **dock** doesn't look safe."

Meg rolled her eyes. "Come on, Greg. It's fine!"

Greg tested the **dock** with his foot. Then he got on his hands and knees and crawled slowly toward Meg and the **duckling**.

big dog
Rocket
dock

The big dog bit the **duck**. It has a cut on its **neck**.
Can vets help **ducks**?
bucket
I bet **Rocket's** vet will!

Chapter 3

A Snug **Duck**

Meg reached to **pick** up the **duckling**.

"Meg!" Greg yelped. "Not with your bare hands!"

Meg looked at Greg. "Why not?"

"It's a wild bird," Greg said. "Birds can carry germs. This **duck** might be **sick**."

But Greg . . .
Let's **pick** it up in the **jacket Rocket** had.
I can get it.

flock of ducks

jacket

Meg held the **jacket** and tried to **pick** up the **duckling**. The **duckling** flapped its wings. "**Quack**!"

"Ow!" Meg said. "The **duck pecked** me! This isn't working." Meg looked around. "Did you bring your **backpack**? Maybe we can get it in there."

"But won't the **duck** get scared inside a bag?" Greg asked. "Plus, it might poop on my stuff."

OK.
sticks

duck
bucket

In the snack bucket?
Yes, OK.
Let's dump the snacks on the dock.

Meg and Greg tried gently pushing the **duckling** into the **bucket**.

The **duckling** flapped its wings again. "**Quack**!"

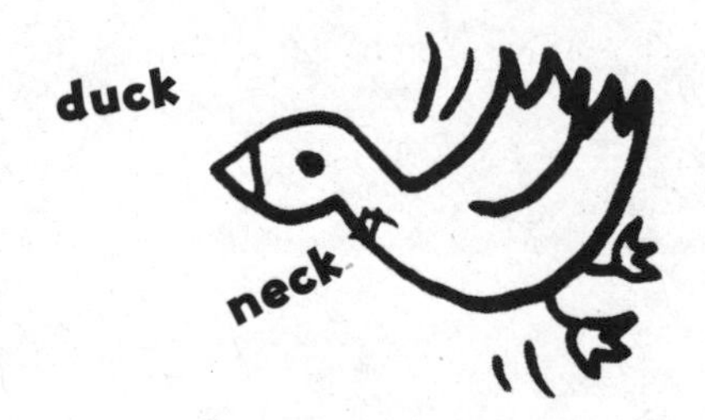

"We need to stop it from flapping," Meg said. "Can we wrap it in something?"

"Like what?" Greg asked. "The **jacket** is too big."

Meg frowned. "I know! We can use one of your **socks**!"

A **sock**?

Yes, we can **tuck** the **duck** up in a **sock**!

black sock
Um, OK.

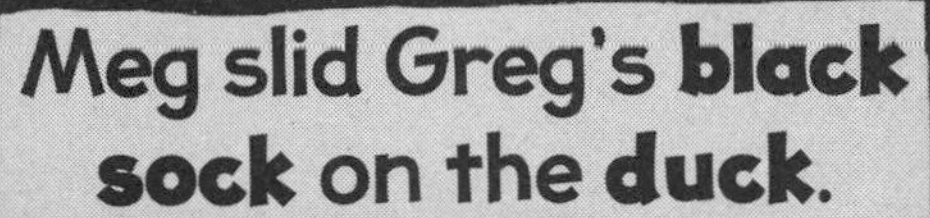
Meg slid Greg's **black sock** on the **duck**.

Snug as a bug in a rug!
Snug as a **duck** in a **sock**!

Wrapped up in the **sock**, the **duckling** relaxed. Meg gently lifted it into the **bucket**.

She held the **bucket** in her arms and sang softly to the **duckling**.

Greg shoved his **sockless** foot **back** into his shoe. He smiled at the **duck**. "I hope you're comfy in my **sock**!"

OK, duck. Off to the vet.
Just let me get Rocket.
bucket
backpack

Rocket!

Rocket?

Chapter 4

Rocket and the Big Dog

Greg called again and again, but **Rocket** didn't come.

"Where is he?" Greg asked. "I hope he's not lost."

Greg walked **back** to the **rocks** on the other side of the pond. Meg went to **check** for **Rocket** at the **dock**.

Is he at the **rocks**?
Not at the **rocks**. Is he **back** at the **dock**?
bucket
Not at the **dock**.

Meg! The mud next to the pond. It has dog **tracks**!
tracks

Greg followed the dog **tracks**. They led into the woods.

Meg took another look at the **duckling's neck**. "Greg, I don't think the **duck** can wait much longer. I'll start walking to the vet while you keep looking for **Rocket**."

Greg frowned. "No, Meg, wait for me. He's got to be here somewhere."

But the duck has to get help! The cut on its neck is bad.
duck
bucket
Greg bit his lip.

Rocket!
Rocket!

Crack!
Snap!

At the sound of **cracking** branches, Greg spun around. **Rocket** ran out of the trees with his tail wagging. Right behind him came the big, **black**-spotted dog, also wagging his tail.

The big dog saw Meg, saw the **duckling** in the **bucket** and dropped his tail between his legs.

Meg looked at the dog. "He doesn't seem like the kind of dog that would hurt a little **duck**," she said. "I wonder why he did that. Maybe he's lost and hungry."

He is still a bad dog. He bit the **duck**.
rocks
Rocket

Well, yes. But if he is lost, we must help him.
Let's get the **duck** *and* the dog to the vet!

Well . . .

Chapter 5

A **Duck** and a Dog in **Luck**

Greg put **Rocket** on his leash and tied the other end around the big, **black**-spotted dog. Greg and the two dogs ran ahead, and Meg walked as fast as she could.

They were in **luck**. The vet's office was still open.

"Hello Greg. Hi **Rocket**," the vet said. "Oh, you found Bandit! His owner came in this morning to put up a lost-dog notice. She will be so happy. Where was he?"

At the pond. He bit a **duck**.
Bandit Lost
We ♥ cats and dogs
Rocket
big dog (Bandit)

He did? A **duck**?
duck in a sock
Yes, on the **neck**.

The vet took the **bucket** from Meg, lifted the **duckling** out and peeled off the **sock**.

"The **sock** was a good idea," the vet said. Meg and Greg grinned.

"It worked well," she continued. "You can also cover a bird's head to help it stay calm. That stops it from **pecking** you too."

The vet glanced at Meg and Greg. "Don't forget to wash your hands. **Ducks** are wild birds."

vet
duck

Is the duck's neck OK?
Yes, it is. The cut just has to mend. A bit of rest will help.
Can it rest back at the pond?

"Not yet." The vet shook her head and smiled. "The **duck** can rest here for a few days. Then you can take it **back** to the pond."

"Thanks!" Greg said. He looked over at Meg, but she was frowning.

"What's wrong?" Greg asked.

"We have no money," Meg said to the vet. "We can't pay you for helping the **duck**."

Greg dug in his **pocket**. He got the zip-**lock** bag of **nickels**.
Yes, we can!
pocket
zip-lock bag

Let's pop the **nickels** in the box to help **sick** animals.
nickels
SICK ANIMAL FUND

"Thanks for helping us," Meg said, waving from the doorway.

"I'll phone you when the **duck** is well enough to go home to its pond," the vet said.

"Bye **duck**! Bye Bandit!" Greg called.

Two weeks later . . .

Greg set the **duck** in the pond. It swam **back** to its **flock**.

flock of ducks
Quack!
Ruff!
Rocket

The End

Turn the page
for more practice
with **ck** words!

ck
match-up

Draw a line from each **ck** word to the correct picture.

Also available at megandgregbooks.com

ck
word ladder

Climb down the ladder by solving the clues and changing just one letter from the previous **ck** word. You'll know you've done it right if the word at the bottom of the ladder matches the one at the top.

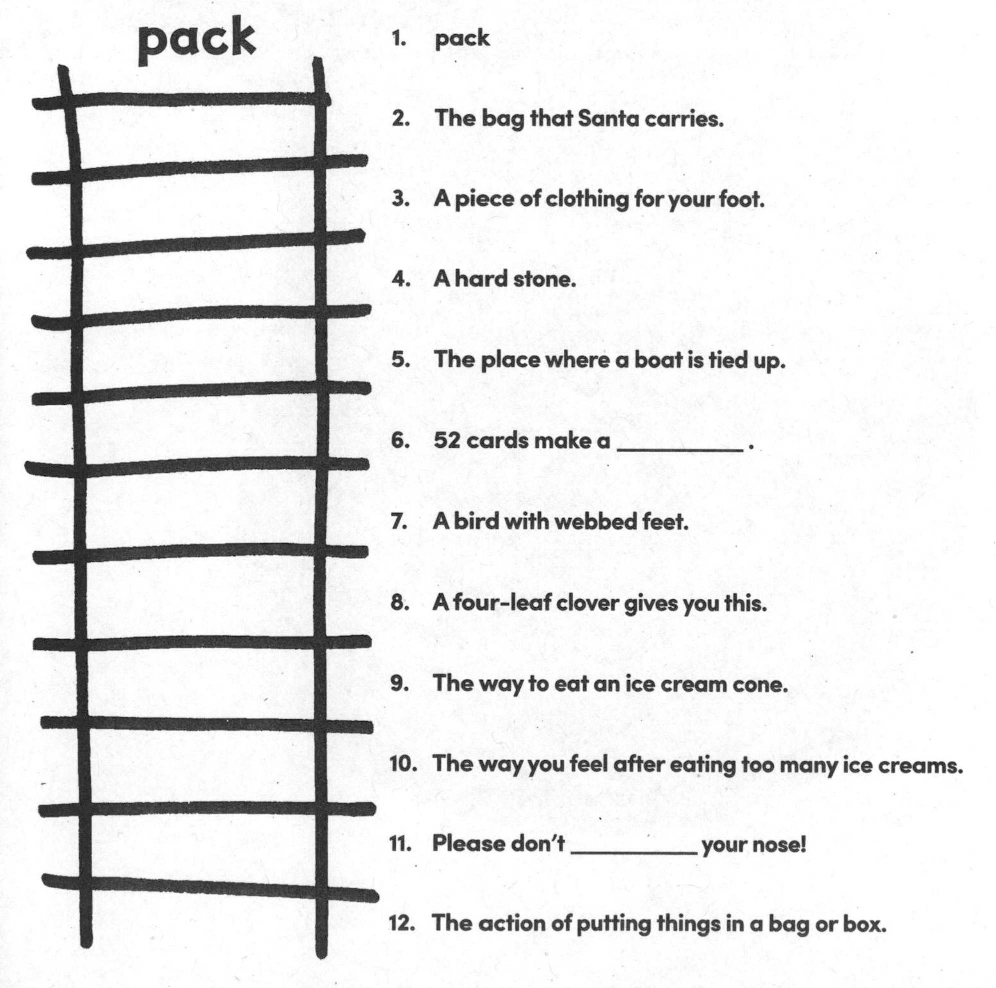

1. **pack**
2. **The bag that Santa carries.**
3. **A piece of clothing for your foot.**
4. **A hard stone.**
5. **The place where a boat is tied up.**
6. **52 cards make a __________ .**
7. **A bird with webbed feet.**
8. **A four-leaf clover gives you this.**
9. **The way to eat an ice cream cone.**
10. **The way you feel after eating too many ice creams.**
11. **Please don't __________ your nose!**
12. **The action of putting things in a bag or box.**

Also available at megandgregbooks.com

This story introduces ***sh*** as in *shop* and *fish*. The letter combination (**phonogram**) ***sh*** is one way in English to spell the sound /sh/. Other ways are ***ch*** in words of French origin (*chef, machine*) and ***ci***, ***ti*** and ***si*** when these letters appear side by side in words with a Latin suffix (*facial, relation, tension*). These other spellings are not included in the kid's text in this story.

The phonogram ***sh*** can appear at the beginning or end of a syllable.

This story focuses on words with the sound /sh/ spelled with ***sh***. It also uses ***ck*** words for continued practice.

For a list of ***sh*** words, including all the ones used in this story, go to megandgregbooks.com.

Swish, the Pet Fish

A story featuring

Chapter 1

Fish in a **Dish**

One morning Greg and Meg were sitting on Greg's bedroom floor. They were making plans for the day.

Greg's mom stopped in the doorway. "**Sasha** and I are leaving for her ballet class. We're taking Rocket with us. We'll be back by noon."

"OK, bye!" Greg said.

"Don't forget it's your turn to clean the **fish** tank," his mom added.

"But Mom," Greg said, "Meg and I want to go to the Tall **Ship** Festival."

"You can still do that," his mom replied. "It **shouldn't** take too long to clean the tank. The box with the net and scrubbing **brush** is in the **shed**."

Greg ran to the **shed** to get the box.

Meg peered into the **fish** tank. "Hi little **fish**."

Greg came back upstairs.

"What do we do first?" Meg asked.

"We lift the tank off the stand and place it in the bathtub," Greg explained. "Then we put the **fish** and some tank water in a **dish**. Next we scrub the tank, add **fresh** water and put the **fish** back in."

"OK, that sounds easy," Meg said.

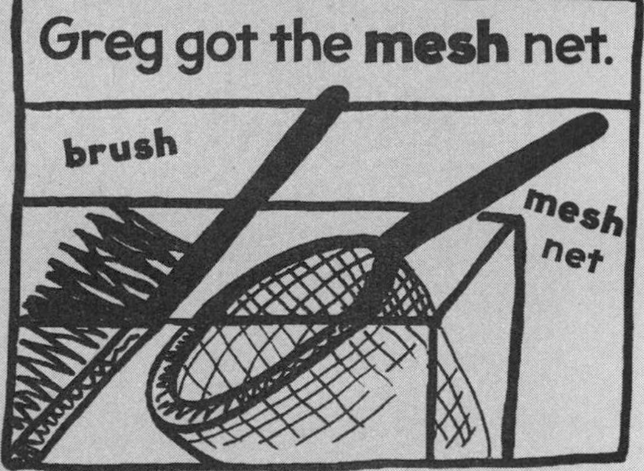

As Meg went to get the **brush, she** hit the **dish**.

Greg managed to catch one **fish** as it flew through the air.

He grabbed the **dish** off the floor, refilled it with water from the tank and slid the **fish** in.

Meg chased the second **fish** as it flopped around the bathtub.

Ack!
Quick! Get the **fish** back in the **dish**!

Got it.
dish
fish

I can't spot the last **fish**!

A **fish** can't just **vanish**!

Greg stared at the **dish** with two **fish**. "We have Dragon and Jade. We've lost **Swish**," he said.

"**She's** got to be here somewhere, Greg," Meg said.

Meg looked on the floor, in the tub and even under the **dish**. Then **she** looked into the bathtub again.

"Greg, I think **Swish** went down the drain!"

Drat!

Swish *did* **vanish**.

Swish the fish

But . . . **Swish** is **Sasha's fish**.

Will **she** be mad?
Mad? Yes, **she** will flip!

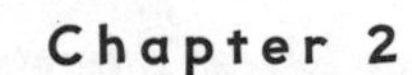

Chapter 2

Fred's **Fish Shop**

"What are we going to do?" Meg asked.

"We need a new **fish**," Greg said.

Meg blinked. "What will we tell **Sasha**?"

"Nothing," Greg said. "We'll get another red-and-black **fish**."

Meg thought for a minute. "Won't **she** notice it's a different **fish**?"

"No. We'll get one that looks *exactly* the same," Greg said.

"OK, then we need a pet **shop**," Meg replied. "Do you know one?"

Well, we got Swish at Ashton Pet Shop...
ASHTON
...but it's shut.
Let's get on the web.
Fish shops in Ashton
Fish shop in Ashton

Fred's Fish Shop in West Plaza.
OK. West Plaza is just 2 blocks up.

Greg grabbed his wallet. "I have six dollars. Do you have any money, Meg?"

Meg put her hands in her pockets. **She** pulled out a five-dollar bill. "How much does a **fish** cost?" **she** asked.

Greg **shrugged**. "No clue."

Meg and Greg biked to West Plaza.

"There's the **fish shop**!" Meg pointed across the street.

Fred's FISH SHOP
Fred's **Fish Shop**!

Um, Greg . . . It sells **fresh fish.** It's not a pet **shop.**
$ $
fresh fish

Drat, drat!

The man in the **fish shop** laughed when he heard Meg and Greg's story.

"I could sell you a live **shrimp** from that tank," he said. "But I doubt your sister would be fooled by it!"

The man added, "You **should** try that new **shop** called Jenkin's."

Is Jenkin's a pet **shop**?
Yes, it is. It will sell **fish**, as well as cats, dogs and rabbits.

$ $
fresh fish
It's at the end of the next block.

Chapter 3

The Cost of a **Fish**

Meg and Greg biked up the street.

Jenkin's Pet **Shop** wasn't hard to find. A huge tank of tropical **fish** filled the front window.

"This looks more like it!" Meg said.

Meg and Greg went in the **shop**.

Meg read the price tags on the other **fish** tanks. "Some **fish** cost less," **she** said. "This one is ten dollars, and here's a **goldfish** for just five dollars."

Greg rolled his eyes. "It's just like **Sasha** to have a super-expensive **fish**. But we have to get the same kind or **she** will know."

"OK, then we need to make some money!" Meg said.

"How do we do that in the next ten minutes?" Greg asked.

?
fish
Let's ask if we can help in the **shop**.

Meg, we can't . . .
Yes, we can! We can help **brush** cats and stuff.
Let's ask!

Greg ducked behind a stack of kitty litter as Meg went up to the **shopkeeper**.

Meg told her their story. "So," Meg asked, "could we pay for half of the **fish** and work for the other half?"

The **shopkeeper** smiled. "Well," **she** said, "which half will you pay for, and which half will you work for?"

Meg grinned as the woman chuckled at her own joke. Greg grinned too. He stepped out from his hiding spot.

"If you each do one job for me," the **shop-keeper** said, "I will be happy to sell you that **fish** for just ten dollars."

Job 1 is to **brush** the cats in the pen . . .
brush

I can **brush** the cats!

. . . and job 2 is to stack the cans on the **shelf**.

cat

OK. I can stack the cans on the **shelf**.

cans

Chapter 4

Splish, Splash!

The **shopkeeper** handed Greg a plastic bag filled with water and the red-and-black **fish**.

"Thank you," he said. Then he looked at the clock on the wall. "Meg! We better **rush**. It's past eleven. My mom said **she** and **Sasha** would be back at noon!"

Best of luck, kids!

I **wish** we had a backpack.
fish
It's OK. The **fish** can sit in the basket.
bag
basket

Greg set the bag in Meg's basket.

OK, let's pedal fast!

Greg zoomed along the bike lane. Meg pedaled as fast as **she** could while keeping her basket steady.

"Almost home, little **fish**!" Meg patted the bag gently.

Greg stopped at a traffic light and looked back. Meg wasn't slowing down.

"Meg, stop!" Greg **shouted**.

Meg looked up and squeezed her brakes. **She** just missed **crashing** into Greg!

"Greg! Why did you stop?"

Meg, it's red!

Is the **fish** OK?

The bottom of the basket is wet. Did the bag rip?

split bag
Splish, splash!

Drat, drat, drat!

Greg frowned. "Meg, you weren't looking where you were going. Now the bag is ripped!"

"I know. I'm sorry," Meg said. "Maybe we can find another bag."

Meg looked around. "Over there! A dog park! Go grab a dog-poop bag."

Greg wrinkled his nose. "A poop bag?"

Meg **shrugged**. "Do you have a better idea?" **she** asked.

OK,
OK.
DOG
splish
splash
splish

Quick!

Greg ran back.
Got a bag?
Yes. Is the **fish** still OK?
She is, but let's get the bag on fast.

OK!
Back in the basket.

Chapter 5

Swish and **Swish**

Meg and Greg dumped their bikes in front of Greg's house and raced upstairs.

"Here you go, little **fish**!" Meg said.

"Welcome to your new home," Greg said.

Greg lowered the bag into the **fish** tank and let the new **Swish** swim out to meet Jade and Dragon.

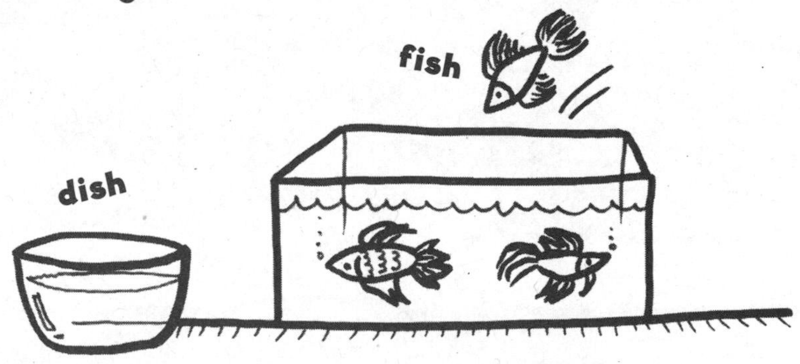

"Perfect! **She** looks just like the first **Swish**!" Greg said.

"I hope the first **Swish** is happy in her new home in the sea," Meg said.

Let's get the **fish** back on the stand.

Slam!

Mom's back!
Quick! Grab the **mesh** net.

And the **dish**!
mesh net
brush
dish

When the front door opened, Greg and Meg were sitting at the bottom of the stairs.

"Hi kids," said Greg's mom. "How was the Tall **Ship** Festival?"

"We didn't go," Greg said.

His mom looked surprised. "Why not?"

Greg **shrugged**. "We were busy with the **fish**."

"Wow. *That* **shouldn't** have taken all morning," **Sasha** said. **She pushed** past them and went up the stairs and into the bathroom.

Sasha slammed the door, and . . .

MOM!!!
Sasha?

Swish is in the . . .
Swish 1

fish

But Swish is in the . . .
Swish 2

Greg?!

Sasha
Swish 1

The End

Turn the page for more practice with sh words!

sh crossword

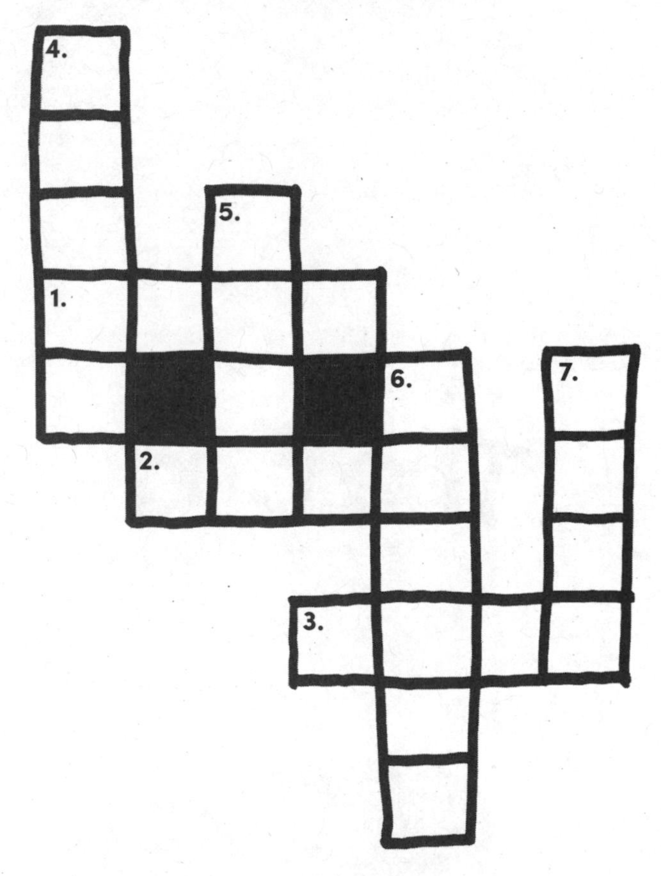

Across →

1. A big boat.
2. Another word for store.
3. Another word for money.

Down ↓

4. The tool you use to untangle hair.
5. Before you blow out your birthday candles, make a _____.
6. The sound a rock makes when you drop it into water.
7. Give the cat a _____ of milk to drink.

Also available at megandgregbooks.com

sh
word wheel

How many words can you think of using letters from the wheel?
Every word must include **sh**.

This story introduces ***ch*** as in *chin* and *lunch*. The letter combination (**phonogram**) ***ch*** is one way in English to spell the sound /ch/. Other ways are ***tch*** when the sound occurs directly after a short vowel (*match, fetch*) and ***tu*** when these letters appear side by side in words with a Latin suffix (*temperature, moisture*). These other spellings are not included in the kid's text in this story. (Note that ***tch*** will be introduced in *Meg and Greg* Book 2.)

The phonogram ***ch*** can appear at the beginning or end of a syllable. Note that ***ch*** can also be used to spell different sounds: /k/ (*echo*) and /sh/ (*chef*).

This story focuses on words with the sound /ch/ spelled with ***ch***. It also includes ***ck*** and ***sh*** words for continued practice.

For a list of ***ch*** words, including all the ones used in this story, go to megandgregbooks.com.

At Chapman Ranch

A story featuring

Chapter 1

Up a Hill and Back

Greg rubbed his horse's nose. "I'm going to miss you, **Chestnut**!"

Meg and Greg were on vacation at Meg's aunt and uncle's **ranch.**

"This week has gone by so fast," Meg said. "I'll miss all the animals—and Aunt Liz and Uncle **Chad**."

"Me too!" Greg said. "Learning to ride a horse has been the best!"

Black Jack
Let's do 1 last trip on **Chestnut** and Black Jack.
Chestnut

OK. Can we visit Glass Pond?

Yes. **Chestnut** and Black Jack can **chomp** on the grass next to the pond.

Chapman Ranch
Let's **check** if it's OK.

Meg waved up at the window. Aunt Liz opened it.

"Can we take the horses to Glass Pond?" Meg asked.

"That's a great idea!" Aunt Liz replied. "**Chad** and I won't join you. We're going into town."

"Great, thanks!" Meg said. "Anything you'd like us to do before we go?"

"Yes, please. Can you visit **Stench** in the pigpen? Make sure she has enough food."

OK, we can **check** on **Stench.**

We will be back at **lunch**, OK?

Yes. **Chad** and I will pick up fish and **chips**.
Yum! I ♡ fish and **chips**!
Chestnut
Black Jack

Meg **checked Stench's** food bucket. Then she put on her **chaps**. She jumped onto Black Jack and took off.

Greg and **Chestnut** trotted after her. "Wait up, Meg!" Greg shouted. "I can't ride as fast as you!"

Meg slowed down and looked back. "Come on!"

The trail wound behind the **ranch** and up a steep hill.

"We're almost at the top," Meg said.

Greg trotted behind Meg. He was getting more and more confident with **each** ride.

Meg and Greg slid off the animals' backs.
Meg got a bag of snacks to **munch** on.

Chapter 2

Back to the **Ranch**

Greg looked where Meg was pointing. He saw a cloud of smoke rising into the air.

"Is that a campfire?" Greg asked.

"I'm not sure," Meg said. "I don't think there's a campsite over there."

Meg and Greg stared at the smoke. It rose higher and higher.

"You know what, Greg?" Meg said. "I have a **hunch** that it's a wildfire!"

Meg climbed onto Black Jack. "We need to call the wildfire hotline. Let's get back to the **ranch**!"

But the pond...
We can't, Greg.

Just a quick swim?

We can't risk it. Let's get back to the **ranch**!
Black Jack

But . . .
Chestnut
Chestnut can smell the grass at the pond!

Greg. Stop the **chit-chat**!

Meg got to the **ranch** first. She jumped off Black Jack and tied his reins to a post. Then she looked back. Greg and **Chestnut** were trotting across the field. Behind him, the smoke was getting thicker.

Meg dashed inside the house and found the wildfire-hotline number. Then she got the phone off the **chest** in the hall. She put the phone to her ear, but the line was dead!

Greg ran in.
chaps

punch!
punch!

Is it OK, Meg?
Greg, **check** the plug. Is it in?

Yup, it's in.
plug
chest

Drat! The **ranch** is cut off.

Greg ran to the window. "The fire is getting bigger and closer. What do we do now?"

Meg rubbed her **chin**. "We'd better get off the **ranch**. And we need to take all the animals with us."

Greg gasped. "Take the animals?"

"Yes, we can take them to my uncle Jim. He lives across the river at Hilltop **Ranch**," Meg said. "The animals will be safe there. My aunt and uncle did that once before."

"But there are so many animals!" Greg said. "Two horses, two dogs, two **chickens**, lots of cats . . ."

Just 3 cats.

And the pig, and the **chicks**.

chicks
cats
Black Jack
Chestnut
chickens
dogs
pig

It's a lot, but let's get on it. **Chop, chop!**
chest

Chapter 3

Chickens Can't Jump!

Greg followed Meg back outside. The horses were **chewing** grass. The two dogs lay sleeping near the toolshed.

Meg ducked inside the shed. She came back out with a stack of carrier boxes.

"Here," she said. "Aunt Liz uses these boxes to take the cats to the vet. Can you get the **chicks** into one of them? I'll find the three cats."

Greg got the **chicks** in a box. He set it in the sun. Meg got the cats.
Let's get **Stench** in a box next.
The pig? Will she fit in a cat box?
box
pig

Let's **check**. She is still a piglet.
box

chaps

She fits! But not an **inch** left!

Just the **chickens** to get.

Greg peered inside the **chicken** coop. "Where are Red and **Chopstick**?"

"Oh no!" Meg cried. "The **chickens** flew up to that tree **branch**!"

"How do we get them down?" Greg asked.

Red
Red! Chopstick! Get off the branch!
branch
Chopstick
Jump!

Chickens can't jump.

OK. Flap!

Cluck! Cluck! Cluck?
chickens

Next plan, Meg?

Meg stared up at the **chickens**. "Somebody will have to climb up to get Red and **Chopstick** down."

"But . . ." Greg looked at Meg in alarm. "I've never climbed down a tree while carrying a **chicken**."

"Me neither," Meg replied. "But there's a first time for everything. I'll go."

"Be quick!" Greg said. "I can smell the smoke."

"OK," Meg said. "Give me a boost."

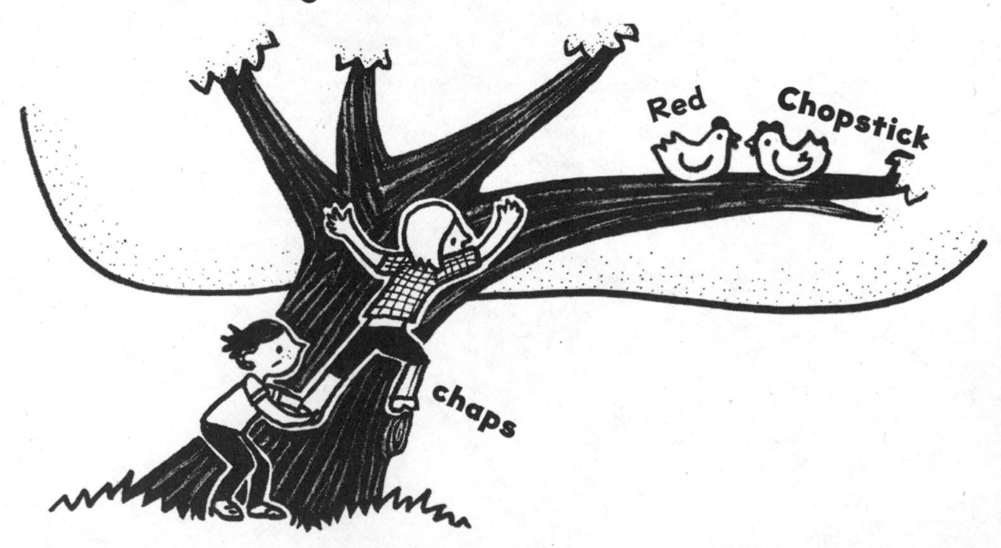

Meg got up to the **chickens'** **branch**.

Red let Meg pick him up, but **Chopstick** went across to the next **branch**.

Flap! Flap! **Chopstick** fell off the **branch**.

Chapter 4

Meg's Plan

Meg and Greg looked at the long line of boxes.

"Now what, Meg?" Greg asked. "How do we get all the boxes to your uncle Jim's **ranch**?"

Meg **chewed** the ends of her hair. She squinted at the smoky sky.

Got it!

The **chuck** wagon!
chaps

A **chuck** wagon? Will the animals fit?

Let's **check**.
Help me get it.

Greg and the dogs followed Meg across the yard toward the barn.

"It's here," Meg said.

"Oh, *that*'s a **chuck** wagon!" Greg said. "It looks like your aunt and uncle never use it."

Meg bit her lip. "I think it's our best bet. Black Jack and I can pull it. You and **Chestnut** can ride behind us."

Meg grabbed the front of the wagon and pulled. It didn't budge.

Greg, help me.

Greg went to the back of the **chuck** wagon.

It's stuck in a **bunch** of grass.
Let's get Black Jack to help.

1, 2, 3, tug!

1, 2, 3, tug!
Black Jack
dogs

Meg led Black Jack around the barn. The wagon creaked, but Black Jack pulled it easily.

"All the wheels seem OK," Greg said.

"Perfect. Let's load up the wagon and get off this **ranch**," Meg said. She glanced at the sky again. "We'd better hurry up."

"Yes, let's hurry up," Greg said. "I'm hungry. I need **lunch**!"

"**Lunch**?" Meg shot Greg a look. "How can you think of food now? We're trying to save the animals!"

Meg got in the wagon.
Pass me a box, Greg.
1 box of **chicks**.
2 **chickens**. 3 cats. And 1 p... p... pig.

Stench, sit still!

Crunch
Bam!
Slam!
Meg!

Stench! Bad pig.
pig
box
wagon

Chapter 5

Greg Steps Up

Meg was crying. She sat **hunched** over.

"What hurts?" Greg asked.

Meg sobbed, "My ankle."

"Can you stand on it?" Greg asked. "Let's **check**."

Meg **flinched**. "No. It really hurts. Now what are we going to do?"

Greg looked at the sky. The sun was glowing orange through the smoke. He took a deep breath.

OK, Meg. Get up in the wagon. I can help.

Sit on the **bench**.

I can get a blanket to prop up the bad leg.
Ok. **Check** the big **chest** at the back of the shed.

shed
dog

Greg placed a rolled-up blanket underneath Meg's leg. He wedged the piglet's box in beside her. Then he untied **Chestnut** from the post.

"Here, Meg." Greg handed her **Chestnut's** reins to hold.

Greg went to Black Jack. He was waiting patiently in front of the **chuck** wagon. Greg whispered in the horse's ear. "It's up to you and me now, boy."

Black Jack flicked his ears.

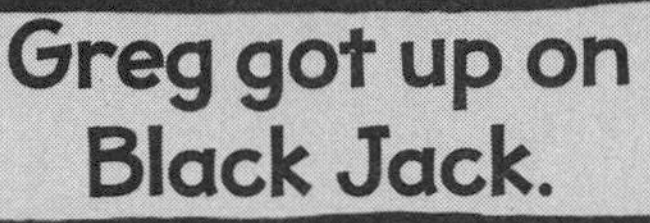
Greg got up on Black Jack.

Got **Chestnut**, Meg?

Yup!

Chestnut
OK, to Hilltop **Ranch**!

I can do it, I can do it.

Black Jack strained to get the **chuck** wagon rolling. Greg clung to the reins. The wagon creaked and swayed from side to side. It rolled through the **ranch** gate to the main road.

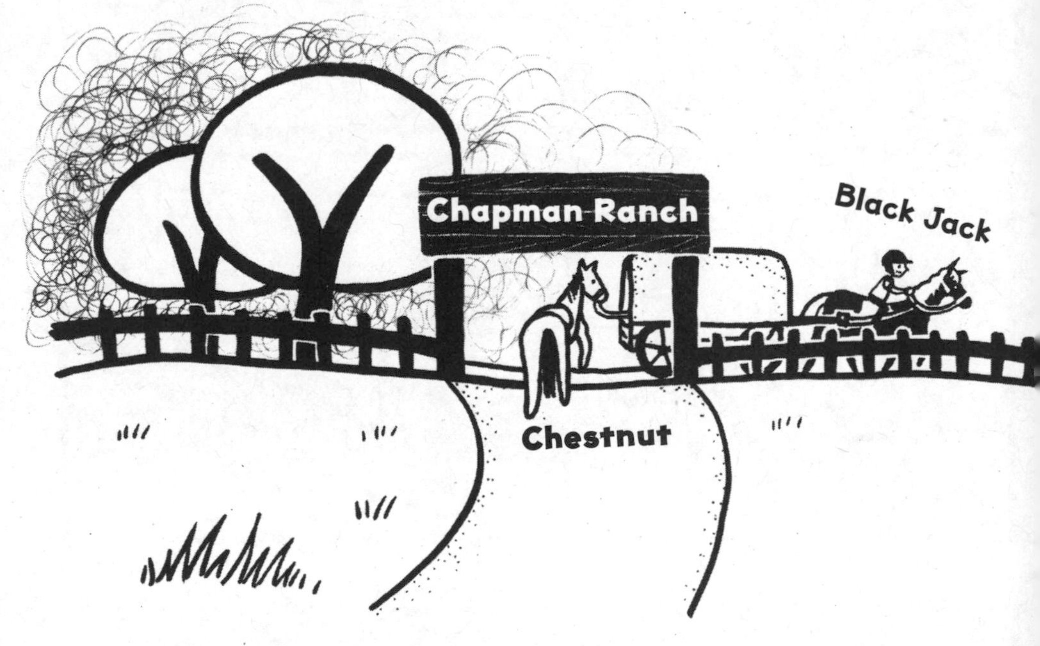

Every time the wagon hit a bump, the cats meowed, the **chickens** squawked, the piglet grunted and Meg **flinched**. In the distance, fire sirens wailed.

Just as the **chuck** wagon got to the top of the last hill, a truck went past.

Chapter 6

Hilltop **Ranch** at Last

The truck stopped and backed up. Aunt Liz leaned out the window. "Kids! Thank goodness you're safe! There's a wildfire!"

"We know," Meg said. "We . . ."

Aunt Liz interrupted. "What are you doing in the **chuck** wagon?"

"This is no time for fun and games!" Uncle **Chad** added. "There's a wildfire!"

"We know," Greg said. "We tried phoning . . ."

Liz and **Chad** weren't listening.

The truck sped off.

The truck disappeared over the hill.

"They'll be back," Meg said.

Sure enough, a few minutes later the truck came **screeching** back.

Aunt Liz jumped out. "I'm so sorry, kids! You've already got the animals!" She glanced at Meg's leg propped up on the blanket. "What happened to your leg?"

"I fell off the wagon and hurt my ankle," Meg replied.

Aunt Liz frowned and **reached** out. "Let me take a look."

Meg **flinched**. "Don't **touch**! It really hurts."

OK, let's get the hospital to **check** it.
Liz
But the animals . . .

Greg and I can get the animals to Hilltop **Ranch**.
Chad

And can we pick up he fish and **chips**?
It's a plan!

OK, Meg?
OK.

Hilltop **Ranch**
Jim

I ♡ fish and chips!
Liz
Chad
bench

The End

Turn the page
for more practice
with **ch** words!

ch
match-up

Draw a line from the **ch** word to the correct picture.

chaps

Chad

chicken

Stench

chuck wagon

punch, punch

Chestnut

Also available at megandgregbooks.com

ch
word mix up

Find the incorrect **ch** word in these speech bubbles.

Also available at megandgregbooks.com

This story introduces ***th***, which spells the sounds /th/ (unvoiced as in *thin* and *bath*) and /th/ (voiced as in *that* and *mother*). Both pronunciations are used in this story.

On rare occasions, the letter combination (**phonogram**) ***th*** can also be used to spell the sound /t/ (*thyme, Thomas*). Don't be caught out by the letters *t* and *h* appearing together but remaining with their original word (*pothole, hothouse*).

The phonogram ***th*** can appear at the beginning or end of a syllable.

This story focuses on words with the sounds /th/ and /th/ spelled with ***th***. It also includes ***ck***, ***sh*** and ***ch*** words for continued practice.

For a list of ***th*** words, including all the ones used in this story, go to megandgregbooks.com.

Get That Sloth!

A story featuring

Chapter 1

The Amazon **Sloth**

Meg and Greg hopped out of **the** car.

"**Thanks**, Mom," Meg said. "See you later."

The kids ran to **the** ticket **booth** at Planet Fun Animal **Theme** Park. **They** showed **their** passes and raced to **the** Amazon Jungle Zone. **Their** first stop was always to visit Sam, **the three**-toed **sloth**.

Meg and Greg pushed open **the** heavy glass door.

Meg **breathed** in deeply. "I love **this** warm, muggy air."

"Me too," Greg said. "And **that's** how **sloths** like it."

"Let's go different ways," Meg said. "We can see who finds Sam first."

Is **this** a contest?

Yes!

I get **this path**.
OK. **Then** I get **this path**.
moth
Amazon plants

1, 2, 3, run!

path
backpack

Greg ran down his **path**. "Oops!" He nearly bumped into a zookeeper. **The** man was putting out fruit for **the** giant **moths**.

"Whoa!" **the** man said. "Slow down a little, please."

"Sorry, sir." Greg stopped and **then** asked, "Have you seen Sam **the sloth** today?"

"Yes, he's asleep on a branch," **the** man replied. He pointed up at **the** tree canopy.

"Which tree?" Greg asked.

Greg went **with** Meg up **the path**.

Greg looked at **the** treetops. He couldn't see **the sloth's thick** brown fur.

"Right **there**, Greg!" Meg said. "Below **that** open window. **The** one covered **with** netting."

The sloth lifted his head.

"Now I see him!" Greg said.

Sam **the sloth** stretched his front legs. One of his claws snagged **the** netting. Meg and Greg watched as he tugged once . . . twice . . . **three** times. On his **third** tug, **the** netting came free.

"Uh-oh," Meg said.

Sam sniffed at **the** open window. He stuck his head outside. **Then** he started pulling himself out onto **the** glass roof.

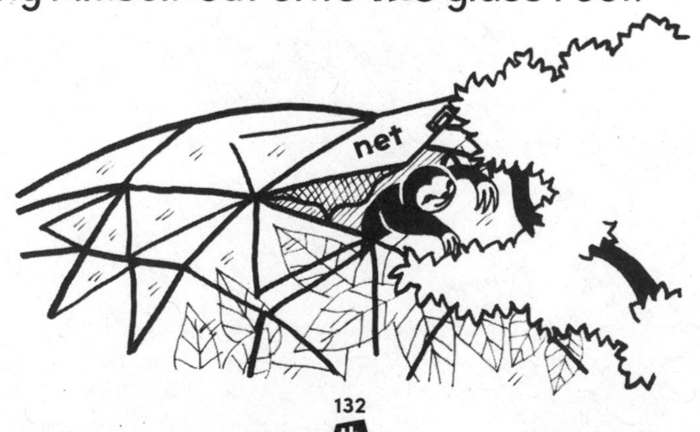

Greg ran to get **the** man, but he had left.

Chapter 2

Sam **the Sloth** Gets Wet

Meg and Greg watched Sam crawl across **the** glass roof.

"What should we do?" Meg asked.

Before Greg could answer, a door opened from behind a fig tree. **The moth** man stepped out **with** a bucket.

"Sam **the sloth** climbed out **that** window!" Meg cried.

She looked up. "And now he's gone!"

The moth man chuckled. "Oh, I don't **think** so. **That** window can't open more **than** a crack."

"But we saw him on **the** roof!" Greg said.

"**That** was probably just a squirrel," **the moth** man said. "Keep looking, kids!" He turned and walked away toward **the** fishpond.

This is nuts.
If we can't get the moth man's help, then it is up to us.

Yup.
Let's get that sloth back!

Maps
Grab a map off that stack.

Meg and Greg looked at **the** map of Planet Fun.

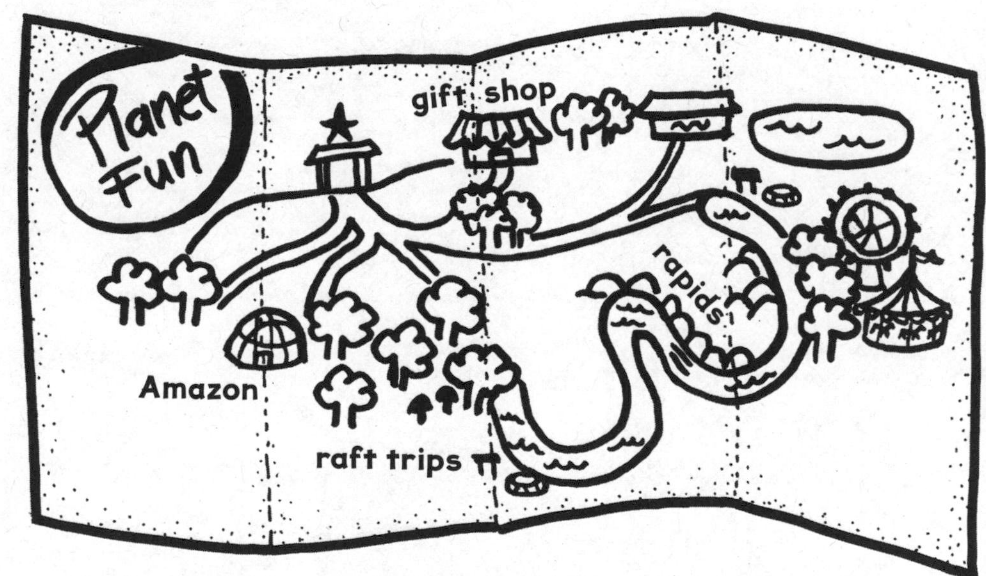

Greg pointed to **the** picture of a glass dome. "**This** is **the** Amazon Zone."

"Right," Meg said. She pointed to a **thicket** of trees next to the dome "Sam was heading **this** way."

"**The** Enchanted Forest and Lazy River are over **there**," Greg said. He stuffed **the** map into his pocket. "Let's find **that sloth**!"

Meg and Greg ran past **the** man as he fed **the** fish at **the** pond.

Meg and Greg left **the** Amazon Zone.

"Wow, it's so cold out here!" Meg said.

Greg shivered. "I hope Sam is OK in **the** colder air."

Meg and Greg ran toward **the** Enchanted Forest. **They** scanned **the** treetops.

"I don't see him!" Greg said.

He must be hidden up top.
branch

Just **then** Sam fell off a branch.

Splash!

Sam!

That's Sam **the sloth**?
Yes, but . . . can he swim?
Sam **the** **sloth**

Chapter 3

Get **That Sloth**!

Meg and Greg ran to **the** edge of **the** Lazy River.

"**Sloths** are good swimmers. Look how fast he can go!" Greg said.

"Sam! Come back!" Meg shouted. She turned to Greg. "He's moving so fast! How can we get to him?"

"Too bad it's so cold today. Nobody is floating down **the** river," Greg said. "It would be easy to grab Sam from a raft."

Sam **the** sloth

Meg and Greg ran up **the path** to **the** stack of rafts.

Thud! Meg **threw** her backpack into **the** raft. **Then** she leaped in.

"Careful, Meg!" Greg cried. "Keep **the** raft still so I can get in."

"Come on, Greg!" Meg turned to look down **the** river. "Quick! Sam is almost around **that** bend. I **think that's** where **the** rapids start."

Greg slid in. Meg **thrust** off, and **the** raft left **the** dock.

At **the** bend, it hit **the** rapids and sped up.

Greg leaned out and grabbed at Sam, but **the** raft was moving too fast.

"Greg!" Meg cried. "You missed him!"

"Sorry," Greg said. "We can paddle back to him."

Meg glanced into **the** bottom of **the** raft. "We don't have paddles!"

"Yes, we do!" Greg started paddling **with** his hands.

Meg frowned. "**The** river current is too strong for **that**." She looked downriver and saw a branch hanging over **the** water.

Greg got **the** branch and held **the** raft still.

Meg held up **the sloth**.

Chapter 4

A **Sloth** in a **Cloth**

Greg let go of **the** branch. **The** raft floated to **the** end of **the** Lazy River. Meg cuddled Sam inside **the cloth** and tried to dry his **thick** fur.

"Sam is shivering," Meg said.

Greg glanced at **the** sky. "Good **thing the** sun is starting to come out!"

Meg nodded. "Yes. But I **think** we should still get him to his warm home as fast as we can. How do we get back to **the** Amazon Zone from here?"

Let me check **the** map.

Yuck.
It's wet . . .
wet map

Get a fresh map!
Sam the sloth

OK. **This path** gets us to **the** gift shop.
map
backpack
Then that path will get us to **the** Amazon.

Greg put **the** raft away while Meg started up **the path**. She held Sam snugly in **the cloth**.

Greg ran to catch up to Meg. **The path** turned away from **the** river and into an open meadow.

Whoosh!

"Caw!" A crow swooped at Meg and Sam.

Meg ducked. "Get away!"

Greg waved his arms at **the** crow. "Leave **them** alone!"

A second crow joined **the** first one. **Then** a **third** came, and a **fourth** . . .

Ack!
A **fifth**!

And a **sixth**!

Get lost!

Run to **that thicket**, Meg!

gift shop
thicket
sloth in a cloth
bench

Meg ran toward **the thicket** of trees.

"Caw! Caw!" **The** crows kept swooping at Meg and Sam until **they** were under **the** tree branches.

"**That** was scary!" Meg said.

"**The** crows must have babies nearby," Greg said.

Meg hugged Sam close to her chest. "I'm not going back out **there**!"

"Let me **think**," Greg said. "I can make a flag to wave at **the** crows as we run across **the** meadow."

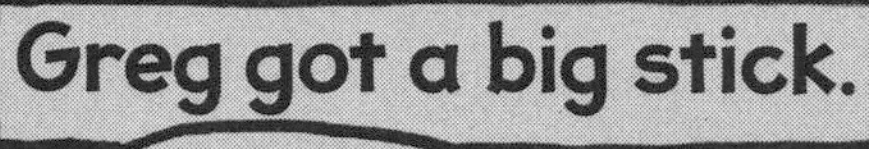
Greg got a big stick.

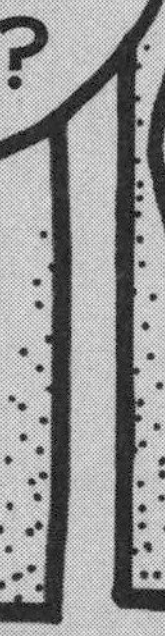
The cloth can be **the** flag.
Can I get it off Sam?
stick

But Sam is snug in **the cloth**.

Well . . .

Stab **the** map **with the** end of **the** stick.

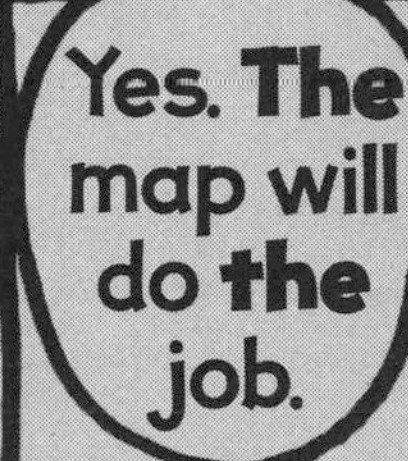
Yes. **The** map will do **the** job.

map

OK, Meg.
flag

1, 2, 3, run!

Chapter 5

Back to **the** Amazon

Meg and Greg ran across **the** meadow and up **the path**. As **they** got near **the** gift shop, Greg ran ahead to find someone to help **them with** Sam. A sign on **the** shop door read "back in 10 minutes."

"Where is everyone?" Greg asked.

"Maybe **they're** out looking for Sam!" Meg said.

Meg and Greg kept going toward **the** Amazon building. **They** heard a voice shouting, "Code **Three**! Code **Three**! Emergency in **the** Amazon!"

Sam is lost!
moth man

Sam is not lost!

Get help to **the** Amazon. **This** instant!

Sam is in **this cloth**!

Sam? **The sloth**? Is he OK?
Yes. But he had a swim and got wet!

The man ran to open **the** door of **the** Amazon Zone. "Quick! Let's get Sam back into **the** warm air."

The man looked at Meg and Greg. "You're **the** kids who were looking for **the sloth** earlier, right?"

"Yes," Meg said. "We saw Sam go **through the** window. We followed him outside, and **then** he ended up in **the** Lazy River."

"**The** Lazy River?" **The** man laughed. "Sam must have wanted a **bath**! I'm sorry I didn't believe you before, kids. **Thank** you for bringing him back safely."

Greg got **the cloth** off Sam **the sloth**.

Meg held him up to a branch.

Sam went up and sat in **the** sun.

The Ashton Sun

Sloth Gets a Bath at Planet Fun

The End

Turn the page for more practice with **th** words!

th

crossword

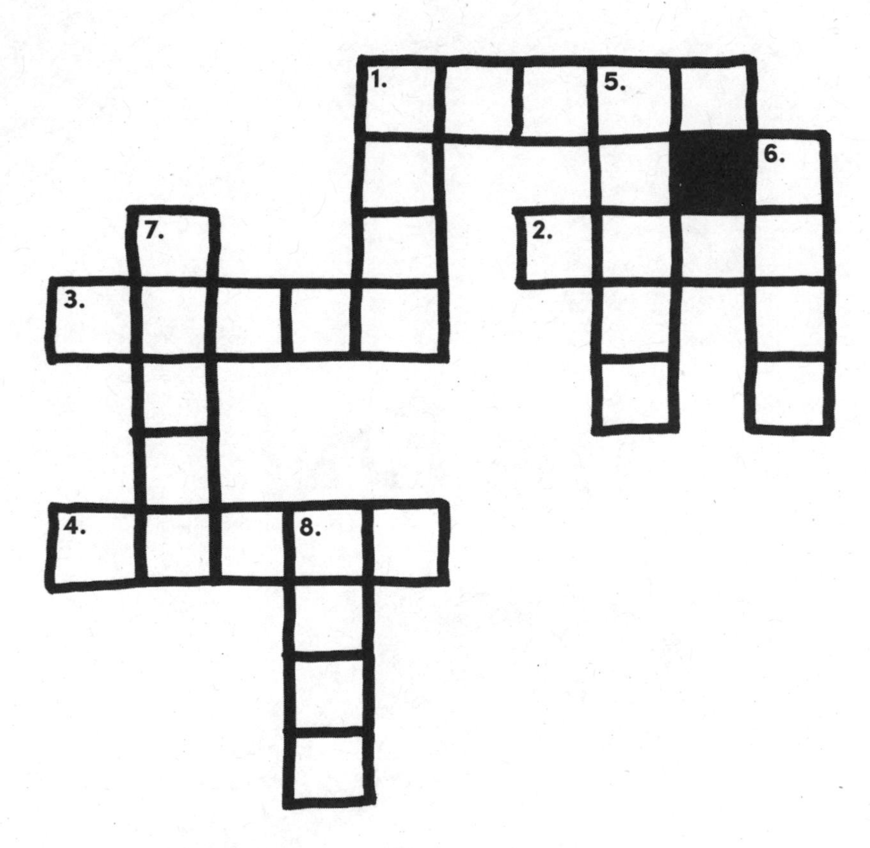

Across →

1. A watery soup.
2. Another word for together.
3. Seventh, eighth, ninth, _____.
4. To bang a table with your fist.

Down ↓

1. When you are dirty, you take a _____.
5. The opposite of thin.
6. Another word for skinny.
7. A measure of how deep something is.
8. At school you add and subtract in _____ class.

Also available at megandgregbooks.com

th
word search

Find the following words in the puzzle.
Words are hidden → and ↓.

g	t	w	r	a	n	c	h	t	c	p	h
c	h	o	p	s	t	i	c	k	l	e	g
u	x	a	s	l	o	t	h	o	o	m	v
b	x	x	z	c	e	k	e	e	t	o	p
a	t	h	i	c	k	e	t	e	h	t	a
t	h	l	e	f	k	l	u	c	k	h	t
h	f	i	s	h	e	r	p	o	f	v	h
j	r	m	r	o	c	k	e	t	l	i	x

bath
cloth
moth
path
sloth
thicket

Bonus words:

chopstick
fish
luck
ranch
rocket

Glossary

ch: A letter combination (**phonogram**) introduced in this book. It is one way in English to spell the sound /ch/ as in *chin* and *lunch*. Other ways are ***tch*** when the sound occurs directly after a short vowel (*match, fetch*) and ***tu*** when these letters appear side by side in words with a Latin suffix (*temperature, moisture*). The letters ***ch*** can also be used to spell different sounds: /k/ (*echo*) and /sh/ (*chef*).

ck: A letter combination (**phonogram**) introduced in this book. It is one way in English to spell the sound /k/. Other ways are ***c*** (*cat*), ***k*** (*kite*), ***ch*** (*echo*) and ***que*** (*antique*). The phonogram ***ck*** only ever comes immediately after a **short vowel**, as in the words *blăck, pĕck, lĭck, rŏck* and *trŭck*.

Consonant: Any letter in the alphabet except for the vowels (***a, e, i, o, u***).

Consonant—basic consonant: A term that refers loosely to the main pronunciation of each consonant. For example, a student who knows the basic consonants will be familiar with the main sound for the letter *c* (/k/ as in *cup*), but not the less frequent sound for the letter *c* (/s/ as in *city*).

Consonant—consonant blend: Two or three consonants appearing at the beginning or end of a syllable. Each consonant sound is pronounced, but the sounds are so close, they seem to be blended or "glued" together. For example, *flop, camp* and *sprint*.

Dyslexia: A term made up of *dys,* meaning "difficult," and *lexis*, meaning "word." Dyslexia tends to be used as a catchall term that describes a range of language-learning difficulties. These can include reading (fluency and comprehension), spelling, written expression, organization skills (executive function) and even some aspects of speech.

Phonogram: Any letter or combination of letters that represents one sound. For example, the sound /k/ can be represented with five different phonograms: ***c*** (*cat*), ***k*** (*kite*), ***ck*** (*stick*), ***ch*** (*echo*) and ***que*** (*antique*).

sh: A letter combination (**phonogram**) introduced in this book. It is one way in English to spell the sound /sh/. Other ways are ***ch*** in words of French origin (*chef, machine*) and ***ci, ti*** and ***si*** when these letters appear side by side in words with a Latin suffix (*facial, relation, tension*).

th: A letter combination (**phonogram**) introduced in this book. It is the only way in English to spell the sounds /th/ (unvoiced as in *thin* and *bath*) and /th/ (voiced as in *that* and *mother*).

Vowel—schwa vowel sound: The way in English that we often pronounce the vowel in an unstressed syllable, like the ***a*** in *yoga*. A vowel pronounced as a schwa sounds similar to /uh/. This is the most common vowel sound in the English language! Any vowel can be pronounced as a schwa: ***a*** in *balloon*, ***e*** in *forgotten*, ***i*** in *pencil*, ***o*** in *person* and ***u*** in *until*.

Vowel—short vowel sound: The way in English that a vowel sounds when we pronounce it for a short time in regular speech. For example, *ăt, nět, pĭg, tŏp* and *ŭp*. The doohicky, called a breve, shows that the vowel is pronounced with a short sound. (Compare with the entry below for **long vowel sound**. Children usually learn the short vowel sounds before the long vowel sounds.)

Vowel—long vowel sound: The way in English that a vowel sounds when we pronounce it for a long time (longer than for short vowel sounds) in regular speech. Long vowel sounds are often represented by a combination of vowels and/or occur at the end of a syllable. For example, *rāin, trēe, bīke, gō* and *mūte*. The horizontal line, called a macron, shows that the vowel is pronounced with a long sound. (Compare with the entry above for **short vowel sound**.)

About the *Meg and Greg* stories

Who are the *Meg and Greg* stories for?

These stories are for children who are struggling to learn how to read because they have dyslexia or another language-based learning difficulty.

We wrote the stories especially for struggling readers who are ages 6 to 9 (approximately grades 2–4), which is a little older than most kids start learning to read. These slightly older learners can understand and appreciate more complex content, but they need it written at a lower reading level. You might see this concept described with the term *hi-lo*.

To make a hi-lo concept work for children at a near-beginner reading level, we designed the *Meg and Greg* stories for shared reading. A buddy reader—an adult or other confident reader—shares the reading with the child who is learning. Each story has five short chapters and is ideal for use in one-on-one or small-group reading sessions.

Aren't there already lots of books for beginning readers?

Yes, but the many leveled readers available for beginners typically don't meet the needs of children with a learning difficulty. These children benefit from learning English incrementally and without spelling exceptions or advanced spellings thrown into the mix.

The *Meg and Greg* stories introduce one letter combination (**phonogram**) at a time. Each story builds on the previous ones by including words with the phonograms already introduced.

How does shared reading work?

Each story has several layers of text so that an adult or buddy reads the part of the story with more complex words and sentences, and the child reads the part of the story with carefully selected words and shorter sentences.

Each story has:

- *Illustration labels* for a child just starting to read or feeling overwhelmed at reading sentences. The labels are single words or short phrases and contain the story's target letter combination (**phonogram**) as much as possible.

- *Kid's text* for a child who has mastered the **basic consonants** and **short vowel sounds** and is ready to read sentences with words using the target phonogram. The kid's text appears on the right-hand page when the book is open to a story. We also used kid's text for all story and chapter titles. As we created the stories, we bound ourselves to a set of rules that controlled the words we were "allowed" to use in the kid's text to make it decodable. If you're interested in these rules, they are listed on our website (megandgregbooks.com).

- *Adult or buddy reader's text* is the most difficult, and it always appears on the left-hand page when the book is open to a story. The buddy text uses longer sentences, a wider vocabulary and some phonograms and other language elements that the child reader has likely not yet learned, but it avoids very difficult words.

A child who is a more advanced reader and simply needs practice with the target phonogram can try reading all three layers of text in the story.

Are there any tips for buddy readers?

Yes! Try these ideas to help the child you're reading with:

- Keep the list of tricky words handy for the child to refer to when reading (see the table on the opposite page).
- Before starting to read a story, have the child read the story title and each chapter title (in the table of contents). Ask them to predict what the story might be about.
- Before starting a story, write down a list of all the words the child might not be familiar with and review them together.
- Before you read a page of buddy text, have the child point out all the words with the target letter combination (**phonogram**) on the left-hand page of the open book.
- After reading each chapter, have the child speak or write one sentence that uses some of the words from the chapter. Some children might like to draw a picture.

Do the stories use "dyslexia-friendly" features?

Yes. As well as the language features throughout the story, we used design features that some people find helpful for reading:

- The font mimics as closely as possible the shapes of hand-printed letters. Children begin by learning to print letters, so we think it is important for the letter shapes to be familiar. For example, a child learns to print *'a'* not *'a'* and *'g'* not *'g.'*
- The illustration labels are printed in lowercase letters as much as possible because children often learn to recognize and write the lowercase alphabet first. A beginning reader may be less familiar with the uppercase letter shapes.
- The spaces between lines of text and between certain letters are larger than you might see in other books.
- The kid's text is printed on shaded paper to reduce the contrast between text and paper.

What's so tricky about these little words?

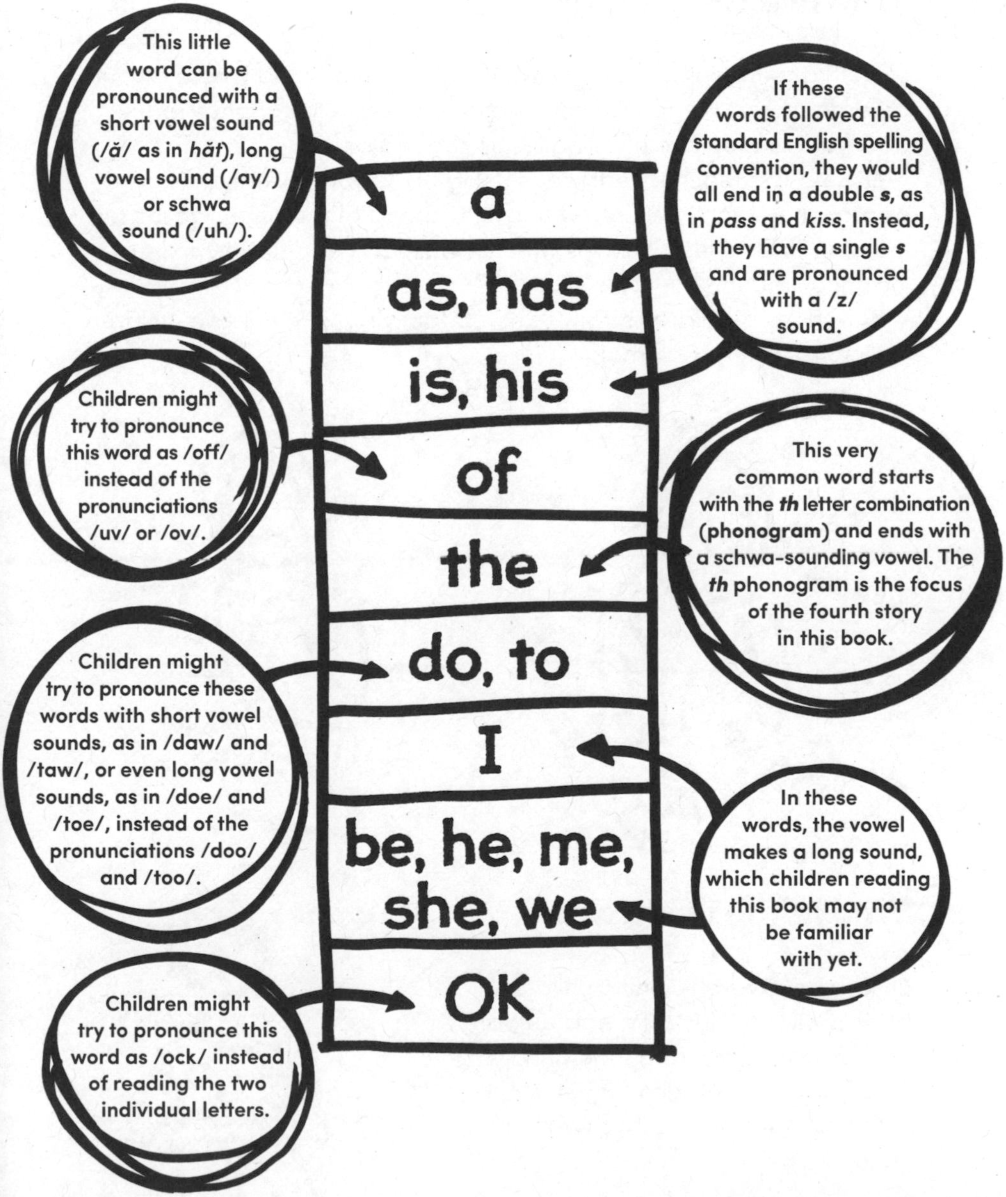

This little word can be pronounced with a short vowel sound (/ă/ as in *hăt*), long vowel sound (/ay/) or schwa sound (/uh/).

a

as, has

is, his

If these words followed the standard English spelling convention, they would all end in a double ***s***, as in *pass* and *kiss*. Instead, they have a single ***s*** and are pronounced with a /z/ sound.

Children might try to pronounce this word as /off/ instead of the pronunciations /uv/ or /ov/.

of

the

This very common word starts with the ***th*** letter combination (phonogram) and ends with a schwa-sounding vowel. The ***th*** phonogram is the focus of the fourth story in this book.

Children might try to pronounce these words with short vowel sounds, as in /daw/ and /taw/, or even long vowel sounds, as in /doe/ and /toe/, instead of the pronunciations /doo/ and /too/.

do, to

I

be, he, me, she, we

In these words, the vowel makes a long sound, which children reading this book may not be familiar with yet.

Children might try to pronounce this word as /ock/ instead of reading the two individual letters.

OK

About the authors and illustrator

Who are the authors?

Elspeth and Rowena are sisters who believe in a world where all children learn to read with confidence *and* have the chance to discover the pleasure of being lost in a good book.

Elspeth is a teacher certified in using the Orton Gillingham approach to teach children with dyslexia and other language-based learning difficulties. She lives with her husband and three children in Vancouver.

Rowena is a children's writer and editor living with her two children in Victoria, British Columbia.

Who is the illustrator?

Elisa is an award-winning children's book designer, illustrator and author with a passion for language and literacy. Originally from Mexico City, she lives with her husband and two children in Vancouver.

Acknowledgments

We owe a huge thank-you to many people for helping us bring this book to life.

So many colleagues, friends, family and children have given us their time. Some have read and commented on the stories in this book, and others have encouraged us and shared advice and ideas. We've tried to include all of you; please forgive us any omissions. Our thanks to Ila Anderson, Lincoln Anderson, Tierra Boorman, Jodi Brown, Katie Brown, Eloise Burns, James Burns, Jordan Burns, Luke Carter, Matthew Carter, Melissa Carter, Tristan Carter, Carolyn Combs, Daniel Cross, Dave Cross, Julia Cross, Janet Elliott, Anne Ellis Clarke, Peter Fairley, Anna Fong, Moira Gardener, Erica Gies, Molly Gordon, Quinton Gordon, Tom Hudock, Wendy Hunt, Meg and Greg Horobin, Susan Kelly, Susan Klein, Roger Lesage, Miranda Longpre, Marilyn Holman, Margaret MacKinnon-Cash, Chelsey Muscamp, Robin Norquay, Leslie O'Hagan, Alexander O'Quinn, Amy O'Quinn, Nikki Penner-Horodyski, Cathy Pledger, Angus Rae, Beverley Rudy, Holly Ryan, Sylvia Sikundar, Ann Skidmore, Anne So, Martine Street, Bettina Tioseco, Christine Tuttle, Marilyn Wardrop, Sharilynn Wardrop, Robyn Wark, Jill Whitehouse, Carol Williams, Andrew Wilson, Genevieve Wilson, Ina Wilson, Madeleine Wilson, Megan Wilson, and numerous students at 44 Sounds Orton Gillingham Learning Studio, Maria Montessori Academy, Prospects Learning Centre and Westside Montessori.

We also appreciate the guidance we received from everyone who helped us prepare the original version of this book and launch it into the world: Laura Backes, Jesse Finkelstein, Zoe Grams, Elisa Gutiérrez, Lenore Hietkamp, Maria Hietkamp, Veronica Knox, Susan Korman, Trevor McMonagle, Kate Moore Hermes, Jorge Rocha and Carra Simpson.

We also thank Sarah Harvey for introducing us and this book to Liz Kemp, an editor at Orca Book Publishers, and we thank Liz, Ruth Linka and Andrew Wooldridge for seeing the potential for the *Meg and Greg* books by taking them on as Orca publications.

And thank you, our readers, for joining Meg and Greg on their adventures. We hope you enjoyed reading the stories as much as we enjoyed creating them!